Visages du Canada

To Shirley Ines bun
with best Wishes
cordialement
Marcoti Pouliot
2.23.96

VISAGES DU CANADA

COLLECTION DE PHOTOGRAPHIES

FORD DU CANADA

FACES OF CANADA

A FORD OF CANADA

PHOTOGRAPHIC COLLECTION

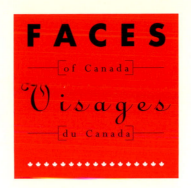

VISAGES DU CANADA

COLLECTION DE PHOTOGRAPHIES

FORD DU CANADA

FACES OF CANADA

A FORD OF CANADA

PHOTOGRAPHIC COLLECTION

CONÇU ET DIRIGÉ PAR
J MARC COTÉ POULIOT

CONCEIVED AND EDITED BY
J MARC COTÉ POULIOT

AVANT-PROPOS DE
GEORGE F. MACDONALD

PROLOGUE BY
DR. GEORGE F. MACDONALD

Préface de Ralph Benmergui

Foreword by Ralph Benmergui

PROJETS PHOTOGRAPHIQUES URBAINS INC.

URBAN PHOTOGRAPHIC PROJECTS, INC.

© Copyright 1992, Projets photographiques urbains inc.
275, rue King est, Bureau 59, Toronto (Ontario) Canada, M5A 1K2

Imprimé au Canada

Projets photographiques urbains inc.

Données de catalogue avant publication (Canada)

J Marc Coté Pouliot

Visages du Canada : collection de photographies

ISBN 0-969643-00-4

Texte en français et en anglais.
Comprend un index.

1.   Canada — Biographies — Portraits
2.   Portraits canadiens
3.   Portraits (photographie)
I.   Coté Pouliot, J Marc
II.   Projets photographiques urbains inc.
III. Titre : Visages du Canada

FC59.F33 1992
779 .2 0971
C92-095020-5E
F1081.F33 1992

© Copyright 1992, Urban Photographic Projects, Inc.
275 King Street East, Suite 59, Toronto, Ontario, Canada, M5A 1K2

Manufactured in Canada

Urban Photographic Projects, Inc.

Canadian Cataloguing in Publication Data

J Marc Coté Pouliot

Faces of Canada: A Photographic Collection

ISBN 0-969643-00-4

Text in French and English.
Includes index.

1.   Canada — Biography — Portraits
2.   Portraits, Canadians
3.   Portrait photography
I.   Coté Pouliot, J Marc
II.   Urban Photographic Projects, Inc.
III. Title: Faces of Canada

FC59.F33 1992
779 .2 0971
C92-095020-5E
F1081.F33 1992

Couverture avant : chemin Rushton, Toronto (Ontario) BOB ANDERSON
Couverture arrière : chemin Tullochgorum, Howick (Québec) JANICE LANG
Troisième de couverture : Parc Lansdowne, Ottawa, (Ontario) TONY GASBORRO

Cover Photograph: Rushton Road, Toronto, Ontario BOB ANDERSON
Back Cover: Tullochgorum Road, Howick, Québec JANICE LANG
End Paper: Lansdowne Park, Ottawa, Ontario TONY GASBORRO

Memories from
and for

different generations:

to Dorothy and Bob
for their generous embrace;

to Kara for her courage,
humour and smile;

to Patrick for the
promises of his future.

La photographie saisit l'instant qui passe et lui confère une éternité que l'heure éphémère, avec toute sa spontanéité, sa beauté et sa passion, ne connaîtra jamais. Voilà pourquoi cet art est privilégié par les personnes portées à la nostalgie. Il leur permet de faire revivre en contemplant une photo précieusement gardée une foule de glorieux souvenirs d'antan. Cependant, la photographie ne représente pas seulement la forme tangible de nos réminiscences : c'est aussi un art qui conserve pour la postérité les caprices du temps et les saisons de la vie, les transformations de notre paysage et la redéfinition de notre caractère national. Selon les mots du photographe et historien canadien Virgil Martin, «Chaque photographie est comme une mince tranche du temps, un instant dans une succession infinie d'instants, rendu unique par le changement perpétuel.»

En cette année où nous célébrons le 125e anniversaire du Canada, prenons le temps d'admirer les qualités de notre pays et d'apprécier ses nombreux aspects positifs. Bien que les Nations Unies aient récemment déclaré que le Canada est le pays qui possède la meilleure qualité de vie, nous tenons parfois pour acquis les nombreux bienfaits que nous avons reçus et dont nous pouvons être très fiers. «Visages du Canada» rend un hommage photographique à toutes les caractéristiques propres aux Canadiens. Ce recueil réaffirme nos identités collectives et notre spectaculaire mosaïque de cultures. Il constitue un mémorial en images des Canadiens de tous les âges et de toutes les sphères de la société, d'un océan à l'autre, à l'occasion du 125e anniversaire du pays. Ces vignettes qui figurent des personnes vaquant à leurs activités quotidiennes viennent confirmer non seulement la remarquable vitalité de notre jeune pays, mais aussi son vaste potentiel et ses aspirations illimitées.

Tout comme nous tournons les pages de cette superbe collection de photographies, passons avec enthousiasme au prochain chapitre de l'histoire du Canada, et mettons l'accent sur ce qui nous unit et non ce qui nous divise. Sir Wilfrid Laurier affirmait que le XXe siècle appartiendrait au Canada; si les années 1900 ne lui ont pas tout à fait donné raison, ne pourrions-nous pas viser cet objectif pour le siècle à venir ?

LE TRÈS HONORABLE RAMON JOHN HNATYSHYN
GOUVERNEUR GÉNÉRAL DU CANADA

Photography freezes the moment in time, grants it an eternity that the ephemeral hour with all its spontaneity, beauty and passion will never know. For this reason, it is the favoured art form of nostalgics who can look back upon a treasured photo and instantly summon a host of golden memories of days gone by. However, photography represents more than the tangible form of our reminiscences: it is an art that records the vagaries of time as well as the changing seasons of our lives, the permutations of our landscape, the redefinition of our national character. In the words of the Canadian photographer and historian, Virgil Martin, "Every photograph is like a thin slice of time, one moment in an infinite succession of moments, each made unique by incessant change."

This year, as we celebrate Canada's 125th Anniversary, let us take the time to admire what is good in our country and to enjoy its many positive aspects. While the United Nations recently declared Canada to be the best country in the world in which to live, we sometimes take for granted the many blessings we have received and in which we can take great pride. "Faces of Canada" is a photographic tribute to all that is special about being Canadian, a reaffirmation of our collective identities and of the spectacular mix of our cultures. It is a visual record of Canadians of all ages and walks of life from coast to coast as the country turns one hundred and twenty-five years old. These vignettes of individuals leading their daily lives confirm not only the tremendous vitality that imbues our young country, but also its vast potential and its energetic aspirations.

As we turn the pages of this superb collection of photographs, let us move on to the next exciting chapter in Canada's history, keeping in mind there is more that unites us than divides us. Sir Wilfrid Laurier said the 20th century belonged to Canada; if his prediction was not quite realized in the 1900s, could we not make this our objective for the next century?

THE RIGHT HONOURABLE RAMON JOHN HNATYSHYN
GOVERNOR GENERAL OF CANADA

C'est avec joie que nous saluons la publication du livre d'art photographique «Visages du Canada», véritable hommage au Canada à l'occasion de son 125ᵉ anniversaire. Ce projet se voulait une invitation à tous les Canadiens, d'où qu'ils soient, à exprimer par le biais de la photographie leur vision des gens de ce pays.

La diversité des visages de ce livre reflète à merveille les diversités sociales et culturelles qui ont façonné le caractère de notre pays au cours de ses 125 années d'histoire. Ce livre ne se veut le porteur d'aucun «message», ni l'écho d'un seul point de vue. Il illustre simplement le regard d'un peuple sur lui-même, portrait kaléidoscopique fascinant d'une époque.

Le but de Canada 125 était de créer des occasions pour les Canadiens de célébrer ensemble le 125ᵉ anniversaire de leur pays. À cet égard, «Visages du Canada» est une belle réussite. Nous sommes fiers d'avoir été le commanditaire moteur de ce projet. Et nous tenons à féliciter tous ceux qui ont contribué au succès de ce portrait souvenir.

It is with great pleasure that we salute the publication of the "Faces of Canada" photographic art book as a tribute to the 125th Anniversary of Canada. This project offered an open invitation to all Canadians, in all parts of the country, to submit unique views of people in their respective communities using the art of photography.

The enthusiastic response and the variety of images in this book represent the diversity of individual backgrounds, character and cultures that define the country on its 125th Anniversary. The beauty of the book is that it does not attempt to convey a "message" or define a point of view. Rather it is a reflection of who we are as Canadians, captured in time by a mosaic of fascinating images.

Canada 125 was established to develop programs to encourage the participation of all Canadians in the celebration of Canada's 125th Anniversary. "Faces of Canada" has been a great success in meeting that objective and we are proud to have served as an initiating sponsor of the project. Congratulations to all those who participated in the success of this visual record of Canada on the occasion of its 125th Anniversary.

CLAUDE DUPRAS, FRANK KING
CO-PRÉSIDENTS / CO-CHAIRMEN

Depuis 1904, Ford du Canada joue un rôle de premier plan dans le développement et la croissance du Canada et dans la vie des Canadiens. Il nous semblait donc tout naturel de contribuer au financement et au succès du projet «Visages du Canada».

À mon avis, il n'existe pas de meilleur moyen de souligner le 125ᵉ anniversaire de notre pays que d'en découvrir le coeur et l'âme à travers les yeux de ceux-là mêmes qui considèrent le Canada comme leur patrie.

C'est avec plaisir que nous ferons don de la collection photographique «Visages du Canada» au Musée canadien des civilisations, aux fins d'archives. J'ose espérer que vous apprécierez pendant longtemps cet ouvrage commémoratif qui célèbre la plus grande richesse du Canada : ses habitants.

Since 1904, Ford of Canada has been involved in the development and growth of Canada and in the lives of its people. It seemed natural that we play an active role in the sponsorship and success of "Faces of Canada".

The project captures Canada's spirit, heart and soul as viewed through the eyes of the people who make it their home, and it has served as a wonderful way to celebrate the country's 125th Anniversary.

Ford of Canada will donate the "Faces of Canada" photographic collection to the Canadian Museum of Civilization for its archives. This book is a timely record of Canada's greatest resource, its people, and I sincerely hope you will enjoy it for years to come.

J. G. O'CONNOR

PRÉSIDENT ET CHEF DE L'EXPLOITATION / PRESIDENT AND CHIEF OPERATING OFFICER

FORD DU CANADA / FORD OF CANADA

AVANT-PROPOS

L'année 1992 aura donné lieu à des festivités, mais aussi à une réflexion profonde sur l'identité canadienne. La réalisation d'un vaste portrait représentant les Canadiens de toutes couches sociales et de toutes souches tombait donc fort à propos. Nous sommes cette année à la croisée des chemins. Quel que soit notre choix, les générations futures considéreront ces photos comme un héritage précieux, tout comme nous sommes aujourd'hui redevables aux pionniers de la photographie de nous avoir transmis des témoignages de notre passé, ajoutant une dimension de plus aux écrits et aux artefacts de notre histoire. La photographie, en saisissant sur le vif un moment, insuffle aux gens un réalisme que les mots et les objets expriment rarement.

La photographie a cette qualité d'être à la fois esthétique et documentaire. Interprétation personnelle du monde, elle présente néanmoins (si elle n'est pas retouchée) une authenticité qui interpelle dans un langage direct celui ou celle qui la regarde. Fait à noter, le projet «Visages du Canada» marque non seulement le 125e anniversaire du pays, mais aussi le centenaire de la reconnaissance du style photographique documentaire. L'idée que la photographie puisse fournir une information objective s'imposait : projet (en 1889) de création d'archives photographiques (considérées il y a un siècle déjà comme des documents inestimables); publication dans les revues des années 1890 de photographies à caractère documentaire; première exposition de photographies dans un musée, à Hambourg en 1893.

L'intérêt de la photographie en tant que témoin de notre société réside en partie dans le fait qu'elle n'est pas réservée à une élite. On a dit de l'appareil-photo qu'il était un instrument de démocratisation. Ouvert à tous les Canadiens, amateurs et professionnels, le concours «Visages du Canada» en est une preuve éloquente. La valeur de ce projet repose justement sur le fait qu'il ne présente pas la vision d'un seul photographe, mais d'un échantillon de la population.

Permettez-moi de féliciter tous ceux et toutes celles dont les photographies ont été retenues par le jury, de même que les Projets photographiques urbains inc. pour la conception et la réalisation de «Visages du Canada», dont ce livre ne constitue qu'un volet. Le Musée canadien des civilisations est heureux d'être associé à cet événement, en tant que l'un des lieux hôtes de l'exposition itinérante de photos choisies et de conservateur de la collection complète des épreuves et négatifs. Il est juste que ces photographies soient intégrées aux collections nationales qui seront conservées pour les Canadiens de demain. Le musée ne fait pas l'éloge des objets, mais bien des gens, en illustrant leur façon de vivre et leur environnement à un moment précis de l'histoire de ce pays.

GEORGE F. MACDONALD
DIRECTEUR EXÉCUTIF
MUSÉE CANADIEN DES CIVILISATIONS

PROLOGUE

In this year of both contemplation and celebration of Canadian identity, it seems very appropriate to compile a portfolio of photographs that — by depicting Canadians from all social strata, different walks of life, and diverse cultural backgrounds — collectively offer a snapshot of "the way we were" in 1992. We stand at the crossroads of change and, whichever route is chosen, fifty or a hundred years from now, Canadians will value these images as part of their heritage, just as we are indebted to the early pioneers of photography for capturing, in patterns of light, records of our past which add an extra dimension to the evidence of texts and artifacts. Photographs evoke the immediacy of social settings, bring us face to face with real people, in a way that words and objects rarely can.

The merit of photography lies in its ability to be at once aesthetic and documentary. It allows for insightful interpretation of the world as perceived by the photographer, and yet there is (in the unretouched photograph) that quality of authenticity which speaks directly to the viewer, calling to mind Keats' formula that "Beauty is truth, truth beauty". Interestingly, the "Faces of Canada" project marks not only the 125th Anniversary of Canadian nationhood, but also a century of documentary photography as a recognized style. The realization that photography could provide objective information is reflected: in the proposal (1889) for the formation of a major archive of photographic records (which were accurately envisaged as being invaluable documents a century hence); in the publication by magazines in the 1890s of photographs for their documentary value, and in the first museum exhibition of photographs in Hamburg in 1893.

The richness of photography as a source of information about social history lies partly in it not being the preserve of those of superior talent or wealth. The camera has rightly been called an instrument of democratization and this is seen in "Faces of Canada", a competition open to all Canadians, whether professional or amateur photographers. In fact, part of the value of the project is that it does not represent the vision of a single photographer, but those of a cross-section of Canadians.

I would like to offer my congratulations to all those whose photographs were selected by the jury, as well as to Urban Photographic Projects, Inc. for their foresight in conceiving and realizing the "Faces of Canada" project, of which this book is only one expression. The Canadian Museum of Civilization is pleased to be associated with the project, as one of the host sites of the travelling exhibit of selected photographs and as the final repository of the full set of prints and negatives. It is fitting that these photographs should become part of the national collections held in trust for future generations of Canadians. Museums are not about objects, they are about people. The photographs are mute, yet powerful, witnesses to people — the way they lived, the environment they inhabited — at a particular point in the history of this country.

DR. GEORGE F. MACDONALD
EXECUTIVE DIRECTOR
CANADIAN MUSEUM OF CIVILIZATION

Terry Fox Run, Regina Pacis Secondary School, Downsview, Ontario

DAVID COOPER / THE TORONTO STAR

Lac Sainte-Anne, Alberta

GEORGE WEBBER

Terry Fox Run, Regina Pacis Secondary School, Downsview, Ontario

DAVID COOPER / THE TORONTO STAR

Variety Village, Danforth Avenue, Scarborough, Ontario
SILVIA PECOTA

The Stockyards, Kitchener, Ontario

KATE WILLIAMS

North Hatley (Québec)

DAVID McCAMMON

Dundurn Park, Hamilton, Ontario

CHRISTOPHER SANKEY

Lansdowne Bingo, Toronto, Ontario

TINNISH ANDERSEN

*La diversité, la richesse des
cultures, le tissu vibrant
de tant de fibres d'humanité,
c'est cela qui rend ce
pays si unique, si merveilleux.*

TOMSON HIGHWAY,
AUTEUR DE THÉATRE

What I'm saying is that it is
this diversity, this richness
of cultures,
this electric mixture of so many
strands of humanity, that makes this
country so unique, so lovable.

TOMSON HIGHWAY,
PLAYWRIGHT

Riverdale Park, Toronto, Ontario

JUDY NISENHOLT

Trout River, Newfoundland

MARY ELLEN McQUAY

Pendrith Lane, Toronto, Ontario

SUSIE KING

Keppoch Beach, Prince Edward Island

CAROL KENNEDY

King Street, Toronto, Ontario
BRUCE HILDEBRAND

Foyer Feldman, Montréal (Québec)

HORACIO PAONE

Rosedale Golf Club, Toronto, Ontario

VINCENZO PIETROPAOLO

Casse-croûte de l'hambourgeois, Verdun (Québec)

DAVID HLYNSKY

Portuguese Bullfighter, Listowel, Ontario
ROBERT SKEOCH

Winterberry Drive, Burlington, Ontario

ANDY DUNCAN

Lac Meech (Québec)

ALEXANDER MEYBOOM

Princess Island, Calgary, Alberta

FRAZER DRYDEN

Mattawa, Ontario

TIM WICKENS

Kincardine Beach, Kincardine, Ontario
SUSIE KING

Cyprus Lake National Park, Georgian Bay, Ontario

ROB ALLEN

*J'ai longtemps gardé en mémoire
l'image très précise du billet
de cinq dollars. Un jour, j'allais au
petit bonheur la chance, du haut de
mes six ans, quand tout à coup j'ai
trouvé un beau billet de cinq dollars
tout neuf. Je me suis mis à rire en
voyant le portrait de Wilfrid Laurier
avec sa coiffure en chou-fleur.
Trente secondes plus tard, j'ai mis
le pied sur un clou rouillé.
Depuis ce jour, douleur et politiciens
ne font qu'un dans mon esprit.*

TIM BOWLING,
JOURNALISTE

Personally, I have long retained
a vivid image of the $5 bill.
As a happy-go-lucky six-year-old,
I once found a crisp new five in the
long grass of a vacant lot and
immediately giggled at the cauliflower
hairdo of Wilfrid Laurier, whose
portrait graced the front.
Approximately 30 seconds later,
I stepped on a rusty nail. From that
day forward, politicians and pain have
been synonymous in my thoughts.

TIM BOWLING,
JOURNALIST

Sarsons Beach, Kelowna, British Columbia

JEREMY ADDINGTON

Markham Fall Fair, Markham, Ontario

VINCENZO PIETROPAOLO

Sainte-Augustine (Québec)

LOUISE ABBOTT

Festival at the Forty, Grimsby, Ontario

CINDY ANDREW

Commodore Ballroom, Vancouver, British Columbia
ROSAMOND NORBURY

Commodore Ballroom, Vancouver, British Columbia
ROSAMOND NORBURY

Croupi Bros. Bakery, Toronto, Ontario

VINCENZO PIETROPAOLO

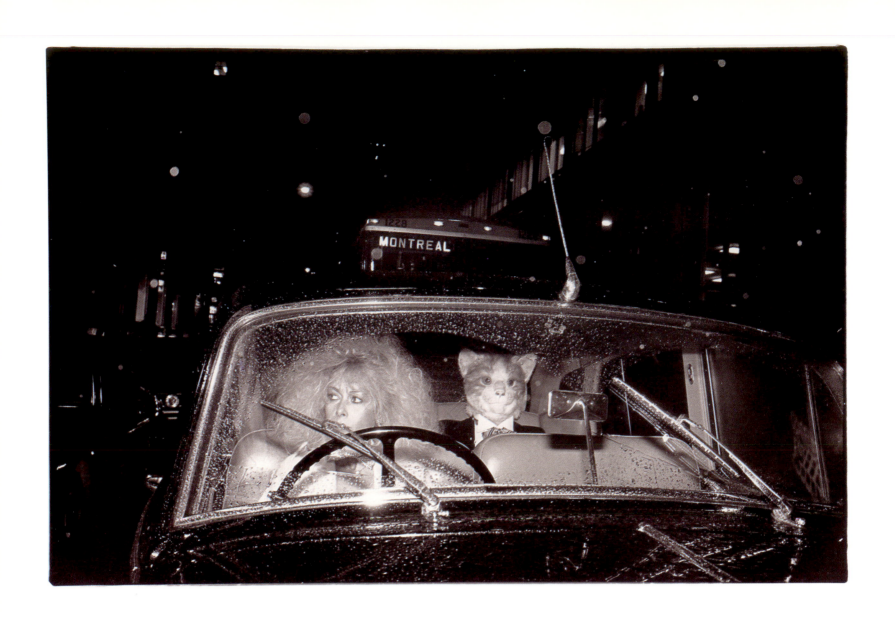

Rue Stanley, Montréal (Québec)
BERTRAND CARRIÈRE

Willard Avenue, Toronto, Ontario

ROB ALLEN

*Quand l'Homme blanc est arrivé,
nous avions la terre et il
avait la Bible. Aujourd'hui, c'est
lui qui a la terre et nous qui
avons la Bible.*

CHEF DAN GEORGE

When the white man came
we had the land
and they had the Bibles; now
they have the land
and we have the Bibles.

CHIEF DAN GEORGE

Welland Avenue, St. Catharines, Ontario
VINCENZO PIETROPAOLO

All Saints Anglican Church, St. Andrews, New Brunswick
EDWARD GAJDEL

Rue Hutchison, Montréal (Québec)

PIERRE BOISCLAIR

Mr. Roy Thomas, Thomasville, Nova Scotia

RENATE DEPPE

Niagara Falls, Ontario

DENIS REDMOND

Harbourfront Playground, Toronto, Ontario

JUDY NISENHOLT

Camp Weselka, Acton, Ontario
EDWARD BURTYNSKY

Aussi Canadien que possible dans
les circonstances actuelles.

GAGNANT D'UN CONCOURS DU MAGA-
ZINE MACLEAN'S OÛ IL FALLAIT TER-
MINER LA PHRASE COMMENÇANT PAR :
AUSSI CANADIEN QUE ...

As Canadian as possible
under the circumstances.

WINNING ENTRY TO A MACLEAN'S
MAGAZINE CHALLENGE TO COMPLETE
THE PHRASE: "AS CANADIAN AS ..."

The Kitchen Bath.

Carol Kennedy

Cabot Trail, Cape Breton Island, Nova Scotia

CAROL KENNEDY

Delton Elementary School, Edmonton, Alberta

STEVE SIMON

Crosby Avenue, Burlington, Ontario

ANDY DUNCAN

Caffè Italia, Montréal (Québec)

HORACIO PAONE

Parc Mandela, Montréal (Québec)

HORACIO PAONE

Rue Bourret, Montréal (Québec)

HORACIO PAONE

CTCUM, Pierrefonds (Québec)

SERGE JONGUÉ

*Le pays où je vis est une terre
douce et tolérante où la
géographie impose la tranquillité
et le sens des limites.
En avion, en train, en voiture ou
en canot, un voyage au Canada est
toujours long pour qui est solitaire.*

MICHAEL BLISS,
ÉCRIVAIN ET PROFESSEUR D'HISTOIRE
CANADIENNE

The country I live in is a gentle
tolerant place, where
geography imposes tranquility
and a sense of limits.
You go on long solitary journeys
in Canada, by plane and train, by car,
by canoe. Lonely voyageurs.

MICHAEL BLISS,
AUTHOR AND PROFESSOR
OF CANADIAN HISTORY

VIA train, Montréal to Halifax, Fredericton, New Brunswick

MARK JOHNSON

Bar Cargo, Montréal (Québec)

BERTRAND CARRIÈRE

VIA Rail Station, Hamilton, Ontario

CHRISTOPHER SANKEY

Diner, Saskatoon, Saskatchewan
BRUCE PATON

Benny's Bagels, Vancouver, British Columbia

BENJAMIN CLINE

Hawksford Crescent, Calgary, Alberta

EDWARD GAJDEL

Cloverdale, British Columbia
ROSAMOND NORBURY

Kensington Market, Toronto, Ontario

CINDY ANDREW

Rue Sherbrooke ouest, Montréal (Québec)

SHELDON LEVY

Kew Beach, Toronto, Ontario

PETER SIBBALD

Canada Place, Vancouver, British Columbia
WAYNE DOUGLAS BUHR

Chatham Township, Kent County, Ontario
LARRY TOWELL.

Loyalist College, Belleville, Ontario

JEFF CHEVRIER

Rue Sainte-Catherine, Montréal (Québec)

DAVID BARBOUR

Dundas Pool Hall, Toronto, Ontario

GEORGE PIMENTEL

Baie des Chaleurs, Bonaventure (Québec)

ALAIN MIVILLE-DESCHÊNES

Euphemia Township, Lambton County, Ontario

LARRY TOWELL

L'amour du pays est de nature
spirituelle.   Or, cette spiritualité
ne naît que de la connaissance
des choses, et ces choses, pour les con-
naître, il faut aller les découvrir
et se familiariser avec elles.

NORRIS McDONALD,
JOURNALISTE

Perhaps love of country is
spiritual, and this spirituality can be
realized only through familiarity,
and in order to be familiar with
something you have to go out and
find it and get to know it.

NORRIS McDONALD,
NEWSPAPERMAN

Remembrance Day, St. John's, Newfoundland

BARBARA SHENSTONE

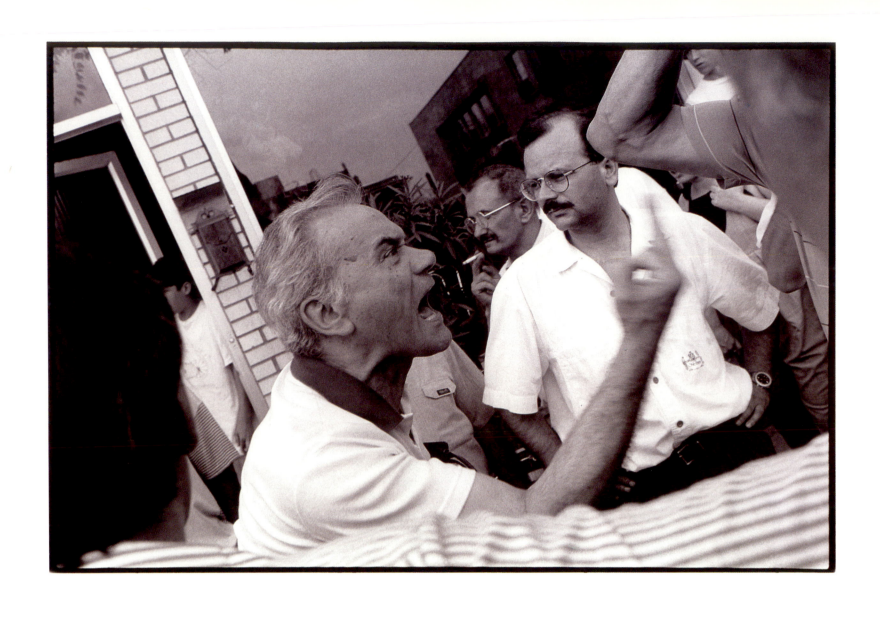

Boulevard Saint-Laurent, Montréal (Québec)

HORACIO PAONE

Red Lake, Ontario

DARYL HARAPIAK

Beacon Hill Park, Victoria, British Columbia

BRETT LOWTHER

Fraser River Park, Vancouver, British Columbia

DARYL CLINE

Shaarei Shomayim Synagogue, North York, Ontario
VINCENZO PIETROPAOLO

Hindu Temple, Brampton, Ontario

ALGIS KEMEZYS

Salmon Bay (Québec)

LOUISE ABBOTT

Zaluski Farm, Waterford, Ontario
VINCENZO PIETROPAOLO

J'ai des amis qui considèrent la notion d'«identité canadienne» aussi contradictoire que celle de «vacances familiales».

MAVOR J. MOORE,
ÉCRIVAIN

I have friends who dismiss 'Canadian identity' as a contradiction in terms, like 'family holiday'.

MAVOR J. MOORE,
WRITER

Sombra Township, Lambton County, Ontario

LARRY TOWELL

Brocket, Alberta

GEORGE WEBBER

Williams Lake, British Columbia

KIRK TOUGAS

In country, near Sheshatshit, Nitassinan, Labrador

PETER SIBBALD

Queen's Quay, Harbourfront, Toronto, Ontario

JOHN MORRISON

Un jour, l'un de mes frères qui

revenait des Prairies

m'a dit : «Là-bas, ils ont deux

saisons : juillet et l'hiver !»

NASSER SHOJANIA,
PATHOLOGISTE

One of my brothers, who had

recently come back

from the Prairies, had told me,

"They have two seasons over there:

July and winter!"

NASSER SHOJANIA,
PATHOLOGIST

Highway 22, North of Cochrane, Alberta

PAT PRICE

Fisgard Street, Victoria, British Columbia

MARY ELLEN McQUAY

Ukranian weavers, Hafford, Saskatchewan

URSULA HELLER

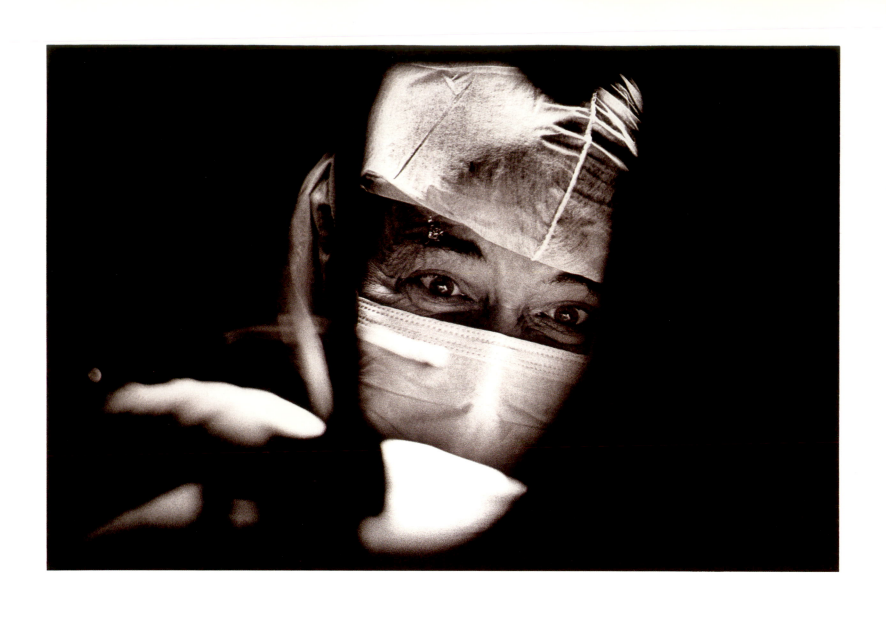

Royal Jubilee Hospital, Victoria, British Columbia

TED GRANT

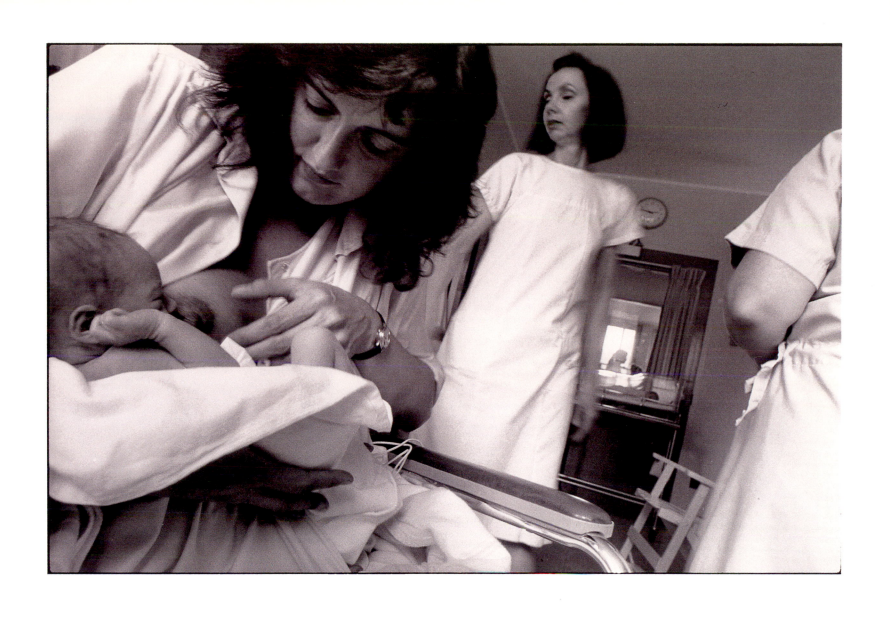

Hôpital Sainte-Justine, Montréal (Québec)

HORACIO PAONE

Gay Day, Church Street, Toronto, Ontario

BLAINE SPEIGEL

Lake Kashagawigamog, Haliburton, Ontario

PETER HORVATH

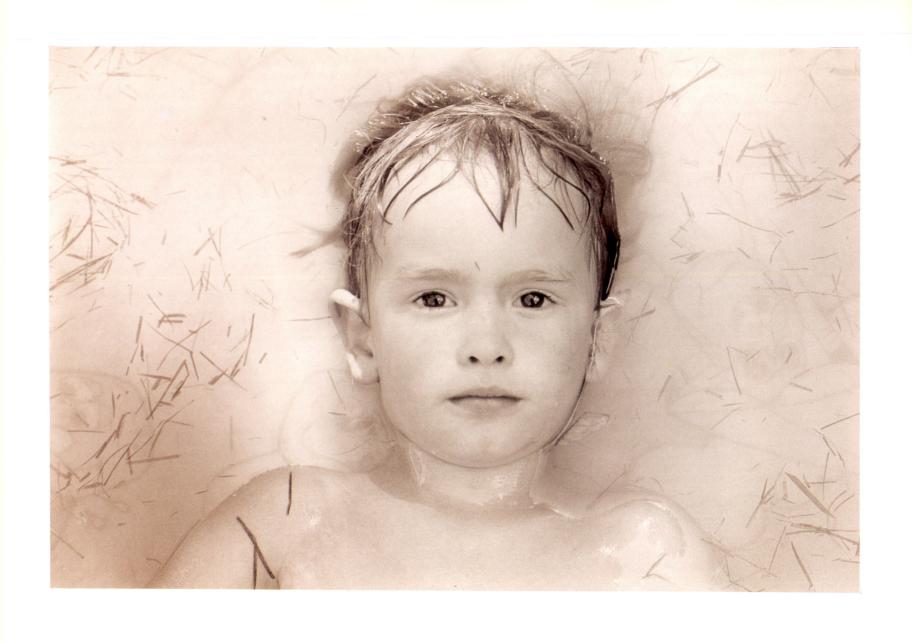

Menno Street, Waterloo, Ontario

JAMES W. STEVENSON

Lingan, Nova Scotia
LAWRENCE CHRISMAS

Dancing Class, Vernon, British Columbia

PAUL MICHAUD

Port de Harrington (Québec)

LOUISE ABBOTT

King Street East, Toronto, Ontario

JEFF CHEVRIER

Boardwalk, The Beaches, Toronto, Ontario

VERONICA HENRI

*Quand un Canadien est seul,
il y a crise d'identité.
Quand ils sont deux, il y a menace
de séparation.*

ERIC KORN,
HISTORIEN BRITANNIQUE, 1917

One Canadian is an
identity crisis, two
make a separatist threat.

ERIC KORN,
BRITISH HISTORIAN, 1917

Sparks Street Mall, Ottawa, Ontario

TONY GASBARRO

Meager Creek Hot Springs, British Columbia

GORDON LAIRD

Macassa Gold Mine, Kirkland Lake, Ontario

LOUIE PALU

Rue Barclay et Côte des Neiges, Montréal (Québec)

HORACIO PAONE

Union Station, Toronto, Ontario

GUNTAR KRAVIS

Crise d'Oka, Kanesatake (Québec)

PETER SIBBALD

Crise d'Oka, Kanesatake (Québec)

PETER SIBBALD

Un Canadien, c'est quelqu'un qui
boit du café brésilien dans
de la porcelaine anglaise et qui grignote
une pâtisserie française dans du
mobilier danois après être allé voir un
film italien avec sa voiture allemande.
Et qui prend son stylo japonais pour
se plaindre à son député que les
Américains mettent la main sur
l'industrie canadienne de l'édition.

CAMPBELL HUGHES,
ÉDITEUR

A Canadian is someone who
drinks Brazilian coffee from an English
tea cup, and munches a French pastry
while sitting on his Danish furniture,
having just come home from an
Italian movie in his German car. He
picks up his Japanese pen and writes to
his member of Parliament to
complain about the American take-over
of the Canadian publishing business.

CAMPBELL HUGHES,
PUBLISHER

Rushton Road, Toronto, Ontario

BOB ANDERSON

Rock Chapel Road, Dundas, Ontario

CHRISTOPHER SANKEY

Green Acres Farm, Caledon, Ontario

DAN HERINGA

Hiawatha Road, Toronto, Ontario

LYNN MURRAY

Avenue Road, Toronto, Ontario

VINCENZO PIETROPAOLO

Rennies Mill Road, St. John's, Newfoundland

NED PRATT

Spadina Road, Toronto, Ontario
ANDREW DANSON

8th Avenue Mall, Calgary, Alberta

GEORGE WEBBER

Rediscovery International, Vancouver, British Columbia

DARYL CLINE

Loon Lake, Saskatchewan

FRANCES ROBSON

Hornby Island, British Columbia

ROBERT CAIN

Entrance, Alberta

OREST SEMCHISHEN

Fête portugaise, Montréal (Québec)

YVES BEAULIEU

The Guild Inn, Scarborough, Ontario

NIKKI DE GROOT

Niagara Falls, Ontario

RAYMOND PARKER

J'aime à penser que ce pays est en quelque sorte un hommage à celui qui est deuxième, à ce qui pousse dans l'ombre. Il faut bien le dire, c'est l'adversité et la diversité qui ont fait la grandeur de ce pays, pas les exploits historiques.

FRANCINE PELLETIER,
JOURNALISTE

I like the idea that this country is something of a tribute to the underdog and the underbrush … let's face it, sheer adversity and diversity are what make this country worthwhile, not historical exploits.

FRANCINE PELLETIER,
JOURNALIST

Kitsilano Pool, Vancouver, British Columbia

STUART McCALL

Annual Gastown International Bicycle Race, Vancouver, British Columbia

ROBERT BLAKE

Coupe du monde, Montréal (Québec)

HORACIO PAONE

Crawford Street, Toronto, Ontario

EDWARD GAJDEL

Lac Elgin (Québec)

BERTRAND CARRIÈRE

Rue Sainte-Catherine est, Montréal (Québec)

DAVID HLYNSKY

Chemin Tullochgorum, Howick (Québec)

JANICE LANG

Ruelle Jeanne-Mance, Montréal (Québec)

PIERRE BOISCLAIR

Fall Fair, Acton, Ontario

GUNTAR KRAVIS

Institut Armand Frappier, Laval-des-Rapides (Québec)

SERGE JONGUÉ

Saigon Palace Restaurant, Toronto, Ontario

PETER SIBBALD

Ce que j'aime du Canada, c'est sa civilité. Il y a dans ce pays une volonté de discuter des problèmes d'une façon relativement polie.

JANE JACOBS,
ÉCRIVAINE

What I love about Canada is its civility. There's a willingness to talk things out — with reasonable politeness.

JANE JACOBS,
AUTHOR

New Dayton, Alberta

GEORGE WEBBER

Sur les menus du monde,
le Canada doit être
considéré comme une vichyssoise :
il est froid, moitié français et
difficile à brasser.

STUART KEATE,
ÉDITEUR ET ÉCRIVAIN

In any world menu, Canada
must be considered
the vichyssoise of nations –
it's cold, half-French,
and difficult to stir.

STUART KEATE,
PUBLISHER AND AUTHOR

INDEX DES PHOTOGRAPHES

INDEX OF PHOTOGRAPHERS

Abbott, Louise, *47, 96, 115*

Addington, Jeremy, *45*

Allen, Rob, *43, 53*

Anderson, Bob, *127*

Andersen, Tinnish, *27*

Andrew, Cindy, *48, 78*

Barbour, David, *84*

Beaulieu, Yves, *139*

Blake, Robert, *144*

Boisclair, Pierre, *57, 150*

Buhr, Wayne Douglas, *81*

Burtynsky, Edward, *61*

Cain, Robert, *137*

Carrière, Bertrand, *52, 72, 147*

Chevrier, Jeff, *83, 116*

Chrismas, Lawrence, *113*

Cline, Benjamin, *75*

Cline, Daryl, *93, 135*

Cooper, David, *22*

Danson, Andrew, *133*

de Groot, Nikki, *140*

Deppe, Renate, *58*

Dryden, Frazer, *40*

Duncan, Andy, *38, 65*

Gajdel, Edward, *56, 76, 146*

Gasbarro, Tony, *119*

Grant, Ted, *108*

Harapiak, Daryl, *91*

Heller, Ursula, *107*

Henri, Veronica, *117*

Heringa, Dan, *129*

Hildebrand, Bruce, *33*

Hlynsky, David, *36, 148*

Hogan Camp, Mary, *19*

Horvath, Peter, *111*

Johnson, Mark, *71*

Jongué, Serge, *69, 152*

Kemezys, Algis, *95*

Kennedy, Carol, *32, 63*

King, Susie, *31, 42*

Kravis, Guntar, *123, 151*

Laird, Gordon, *120*

Lang, Janice, *149*

Levy, Sheldon, *79*

Lowther, Brett, *92*

McCall, Stuart, *143*

McCammon, David, *25*

McQuay, Mary Ellen, *30, 106*

Meyboom, Alexander, *39*

Michaud, Paul, *114*

Miville-Deschênes, Alain, *86*

Morrison, John, *103*

Murray, Lynn, *130*

Nisenholt, Judy, *29, 60*

Norbury, Rosamond, *49, 50, 77*

Palu, Louie, *121*

Paone, Horacio, *34, 66, 67, 68, 90, 109, 122, 145*

Parker, Raymond, 141

Paton, Bruce, 74

Pecota, Silvia, 23

Pietropaolo, Vincenzo, *35, 46, 51, 55, 94, 97, 131*

Pimentel, George, 85

Pratt, Ned , *132*

Price, Pat, *105*

Redmond, Denis, *59*

Robson, Frances, *136*

Sankey, Christopher, *26, 73, 128*

Semchishen, Orest, *138*

Shenstone, Barbara, *89*

Sibbald, Peter, *80, 102, 124, 125, 153*

Simon, Steve, *64*

Skeoch, Robert, *37*

Speigel, Blaine, *110*

Stevenson, James W., *112*

Tougas, Kirk, *101*

Towell, Larry, *82, 87, 99*

Webber, George, *20, 21, 100, 134, 155*

Wickens, Tim, *41*

Williams, Kate, *24*

REMERCIEMENTS

Au nom des membres du comité organisateur, nous souhaitons remercier tout d'abord Son Excellence le très honorable Ramon John Hnatyshyn, Gouverneur général du Canada, d'avoir accepté la présidence d'honneur de Visages du Canada. Son appui dès les premiers moments du projet furent pour nous un grand privilège et une source de motivation.

Visages du Canada a été conçu et réalisé par les Projets photographiques urbains inc., en collaboration avec la Corporation Canada 125.

Visages du Canada n'aurait jamais vu le jour sans l'appui initial de Canada 125 et la générosité de Ford du Canada, Dylex Limitée, la Société canadienne des postes, Air Canada, La Baie, Minolta Canada, les centres commerciaux Cadillac Fairview, BGM Centre de photo, Markborough Properties, Communications Canada, Papiers Inter-Cité, IPI Graphics, Linotext Digital Colour et l'hôtel King Edward.

Pour avoir si gracieusement partagé avec nous leur temps, leur énergie et leur vision, nous remercions les membres du jury du concours : Serge Clément, photographe; Yuri Dojc, photographe; Evergon, artiste et photographe; Sandra Grant Marchand, conservatrice de musée; Dawn Lille Horwitz, professeure; Yvonne Maracle, directrice d'association; Susan McEachern, photographe et professeure; Charles Pachter, artiste; Chick Rice, photographe; Karen Satok, graphiste; et Sandra Semchuck, photographe et professeure. Leur travail tout au long du processus de sélection témoigne de leur amour de la photographie et de leur profond respect pour les oeuvres présentées.

Nous sommes également reconnaissants aux milliers de photographes, amateurs et professionnels, qui, en participant au concours Visages du Canada, nous ont présenté des visions si différentes mais toutes merveilleuses des Canadiens. L'autoportrait que constitue ce livre est tiré des 377 photographies de la collection Visages du Canada, retenues par le jury à partir des 38 782 épreuves inscrites au concours.

Pour leur extraordinaire générosité et leur grande compréhension des exigences d'un tel projet, nous tenons à remercier tout spécialement notre commanditaire principal, Ford du Canada. Nous lui devons en grande partie le succès de l'événement. Merci à James G. O'Connor, Tony Fredo, Ron Dodds, Jean Morin et Anne Bélec.

Nous tenons aussi à souligner le précieux soutien de Claude Dupras, Frank King, Daniel Iannuzzi, Ingrid Saumart et Sylvie Cloutier à la Corporation Canada 125; de Irving Levine, Wayne Bonner, Greg Crombie et John Lemme, à Dylex Limitée; de Dan Campbell, Louise Maffett et Pierre Yves Villeneuve à la Société canadienne des postes; de Jerry Hartman, Barry Agnew, Rick Moore et Bob Keating à La Baie; de l'honorable Perrin Beatty, Alain Gourd, Michael Bourke, Dan Tish et Marc Séguin à Communications Canada; de Peter Sharpe et John Gardner à Cadillac Fairview; de Bob Graham, Ilgvars Broks, David Kingstone et Philippe Gascon à BGM Centre de photo; de Shigeharu Taniuchi, Ted Nakai, Sylvia White et Ken Tatemichi à Minolta Canada; de Neil R. Wood, Blake Hossack et Karen Barrett à Markborough Properties; de Sam Brown à Papiers Inter-Cité; de Dave Miller, Mark Gaudette et Ken Harris à Whyte Hook Papers;

de Dan McGuire à Scheufelen N.A.; de Ron Burtch, Rick Retter, Bob Askin, Dino Martignago et Scott Patterson à IPI Graphics; de Gregor Bingham, Charles Hume, Han Wanders, Jon Barham, Ernie Lee, Thomas Queenville et Jonathan Mitchell à Linotext Digital Colour; de Jacques Dumont à Photo Digest et Photo Sélection; de Gordon Young, Anne Pachal, Dave Roy et Josée Leduc à Air Canada; de George MacDonald, Sylvie Morel, Sandra Lorimer, Linda Morris et Jerry Lewis au Musée canadien des civilisations.

Pour leur collaboration à la mise sur pied du projet, nous remercions sincèrement Ken Hepburn, Martha Langford, Lilian Rayson, Mary Smiley, Ned Ellis, Vivian Farmer, Michèle Gaudette, Lisa Elliott, Doug Paulson, Lorol Byrne Nielsen, Blake Hossak et Michelle Pinard. Pour leur contribution à l'organisation de l'événement, nous ne saurions passer sous silence le travail de Peter Francey, Clark Spencer et Paul Hodgson à Spencer Francey Peters; de Peter Harris et Richard Anthistle à Young & Rubicam; de Frances Matich et Eric Snyder à PPL Marketing Services; de Federick S. Malleau, Reg Hunt, Ken Freek et Michael O'Leary à John Deyell Company; de Paul André Bosc à Château des Charmes Wines; de Sandy McLean et Susan Ferrier à The Globe and Mail; de Karen Seaboyer à CML Communications, Halifax; de Marnie Huckvale à Green and Huckvale, Vancouver; de Katherine Holmes à Holmes Creative Communications, Toronto; de Bill Croke, Carin Robertson, Marisa Salgado, John Higgins et Ashley Farrel à l'hôtel King Edward.

D'autres, encore, ont apporté leur concours à différentes étapes du projet. Qu'il nous soit permis de remercier : l'honorable Donald Johnston, Duke Dickson, Eva Dojc, Mary Jane Finlayson, Gary Beelik, Deborah Upton, David Renouf, Brigitte Lavictoire, Nicole Pelletier, Graziella Malagoni, Renaud Hartzer, John Beck, Dale Pruden, Brian Summers, Blanche McMillan, Linda Harding, Kay Francis, Peter Rudd, Heather Mullin, Stephen Schroeder, Clothilde Bousser, Steve Davenport, Rémy Leduc, Alexander Nicholson, James McMillan, Nicholas Saumart-Dufour, Joëlle Marchand, Wayne Chan, et Barton et Vicki Myers.

Nous aimerions enfin remercier nos plus précieux collaborateurs : Stan Blomberg, dont les qualités de coeur, l'humour et le dévouement ont énormément facilité notre quotidien; Christy McMillan, dont l'extrême gentillesse a donné un coeur à Visages du Canada, et dont la patience et le sens de l'organisation ont permis un suivi exemplaire du livre, de la collection, des photographies et photographes, du laboratoire, des agrandissements et du montage des expositions, et ont fait en sorte que nous restions sains d'esprit; Monique Joly, dont les talents d'écriture ont une fois encore rendu justice à la beauté de la langue française; Karen Satok, conceptrice graphique de projet, dont le travail et la créativité l'ont amenée à réaliser un design de première classe qui va bien au-delà du simple graphisme; Robert Marshall, dont le souci du détail et l'appui indéfectible se sont révélés indispensables. Ensemble, ils ont accompli une grande partie du travail.

J MARC COTÉ POULIOT,
DIRECTEUR DE RÉDACTION

ACKNOWLEDGMENTS

[160]

On behalf of the members of the Organizing Committee, we would first like to thank His Excellency, The Right Honourable Ramon J. Hnatyshyn, Governor General of Canada for his patronage of the Faces of Canada project. His Excellency's support from the beginning and during the development of the project was a great honour and instrumental to our commitment.

The Faces of Canada project was developed and produced by Urban Photographic Projects, Inc. in collaboration with the Canada 125 Corporation.

Faces of Canada could not have been realized without the early support of the Canada 125 Corporation and the generous assistance of the Ford Motor Company of Canada, Dylex Limited, Canada Post, Air Canada, The Bay, Minolta Canada, BGM Colour Laboratories, Cadillac Fairview Shopping Centres, Communications Canada, Markborough Properties, Inter City Papers, IPI Graphics, Linotext Digital Colour and the King Edward Hotel.

For their generous gift of time, spirit and vision to the competition jurying process, we thank photographer Serge Clément, photographer Yuri Dojc, artist and photographer Evergon, museum curator Sandra Grant-Marchand, professor Dawn Lille Horwitz, association director Yvonne Maracle, photographer and teacher Susan McEachern, artist Charles Pachter, photographer Chick Rice, graphic designer Karen Satok and photographer and teacher Sandra Semchuck. Their commitment to both photography and the work of the many different artists was expressed with great clarity and undeterred honesty.

We are truly grateful for the wondrous and varied perceptions of Canadians presented by the thousands of amateur and professional photographers who participated in the Faces of Canada competition. This self-portrait of Canadians was edited from the 377 photographs in the Faces of Canada collection. The collection was created by the Competition Jury from the 38,782 photographs entered in the competition.

For their remarkable generosity and tremendous sensitivity to the project's requirements, we would like to offer special thanks to the Ford Motor Company of Canada whose Principal Sponsorship of the event was key to its success. Thank you James G. O'Connor, Tony Fredo, Ron Dodds, Jean Morin and Anne Bélec.

For their generous assistance throughout the project, we would like to recognize Claude Dupras, Frank King, Daniel Iannuzzi, Ingrid Saumart and Sylvie Cloutier, The Canada 125 Corporation; Irving Levine, Wayne Bonner, Greg Crombie and John Lemme, Dylex Limited; Dan Campbell, Louise Maffett and Pierre Yves Villeneuve, The Canada Post Corporation; Jerry Hartman, Barry Agnew, Rick Moore and Bob Keating, The Bay; The Honourable Perrin Beatty, Alain Gour, Michael Bourke, Dan Tish and Marc Séguin, Communications Canada; Peter Sharpe and John Gardner, The Cadillac Fairview Corporation; Bob Graham, Ilgvars Broks, David Kingstone and Philippe Gascon, BGM Colour Laboratories; Shigeharu Taniuchi, Ted Nakai, Sylvia White and Ken Tatemichi, Minolta Canada; Neil R. Wood, Blake Hossack and Karen Barrett, Markborough Properties; Sam Brown, Inter City Papers; Dave Miller, Mark Gaudette and Ken Harris, Whyte Hook Papers; Dan McGuire, Scheufelen N.A.; Ron Burtch, Rick Retter, Dino Martignago, Bob Askin, Scott Patterson, IPI Graphics; Gregor Bingham,

Charles Hume, Han Wanders, Jon Barham, Ernie Lee, Thomas Queenville and Jonathan Mitchell, Linotext Digital Colour; Jacques Dumont, Photo Digest and Photo Sélection; Gordon Young, Anne Pachal, Dave Roy and Josée Leduc, Air Canada; Dr. George MacDonald, Sylvie Morel, Sandra Lorimer, Linda Morris and Jerry Lewis, The Canadian Museum of Civilization.

For their support in the early stages of the project development, we would particularly like to thank Ken Hepburn, Martha Langford, Lilian Rayson, Mary Smiley, Ned Ellis, Vivian Farmer, Michèle Gaudette, Lisa Elliott, Doug Paulson, Lorol Byrne Nielsen, Blake Hossak and Michelle Pinard. For their support in the organization of the event, we would like to acknowledge the work of Peter Francey, Clark Spencer and Paul Hodgson, Spencer Francey Peters; Peter Harris and Richard Anthistle, Young & Rubicam; Frances Matich and Eric Snyder, PPL Marketing Services; Frederick Malleau, Reg Hunt, Ken Freek and Michael O'Leary, John Deyell Company; Paul André Bosc, Château des Charmes Wines; Sandy MacLean and Susan Ferrier, The Globe and Mail; Judith Allen, Allen & Company, Ottawa; Karen Seaboyer, CML Communications, Halifax; Marnie Huckvale, Green and Huckvale, Vancouver; Katherine Holmes, Holmes Creative Communications, Toronto; Bill Croke, Carin Robertson, Marisa Salgado, John Higgins and Ashley Farrel, the King Edward Hotel.

Others who have helped at various times and in most valuable ways were: The Honourable Donald Johnston, John Robert Colombo, Duke Dickson, Eva Dojc,

Mary Jane Finlayson, Gary Beelik, Deborah Upton, David Renouf, Brigitte Lavictoire, Nicole Pelletier, Graziella Malagoni, Renaud Hartzer, John Beck, Dale Pruden, Brian Summers, Blanche McMillan, Linda Harding, Kay Francis, Peter Rudd, Heather Mullin, Stephen Schroeder, Virginia McCant, Matthew Howe, Alan Calder, Clotilde Bousser, Steve Davenport, Remy Leduc, Alexander Nicholson, James McMillan, Nicholas Saumart-Dufour, Joëlle Marchand, Wayne Chan and Barton and Vicki Myers.

Our most invaluable collaborators were Stan Blomberg whose generosity of heart, sense of humour and dedication to each and every task were instrumental to the day to day operations of the Faces of Canada office; Christy McMillan whose friendliness and kindness with everyone gave Faces of Canada a heart – her incredible patience and tracking system kept the collection, the book, the exhibition, the photographers, the photographs, the laboratory, the blowups, the exhibition system and our sanity in the right order; Monique Joly whose extraordinary writing talent once again ensured that the French texts we publish are worthy of that incredibly beautiful language; Karen Satok whose commitment to design and to the project allowed her to see beyond the Artistic Director – her remarkable talent and creativity was instrumental to all our communications; Robert Marshall whose attention to details in all phases and at every level of the project saved the day and all of us in the process. Together they organized and executed much of the work involved.

J MARC COTÉ POULIOT,
EDITOR

PROJETS PHOTOGRAPHIQUES URBAINS INC.

Les Projets photographiques urbains inc. est une société à but non lucratif qui réunit des gens, peu nombreux certes, mais déterminés à créer des archives photographiques à l'intention des générations futures et, ce faisant, à promouvoir l'art photographique auprès du grand public.

Cet intérêt pour les archives est né d'une expérience de recherche historique effectuée à Montréal à la fin des années 1970. Nous avions alors eu la chance de consulter les archives photographiques Notman du Musée McCord, datant de la fin du XIXe siècle. Les photographies de Notman nous permirent de recréer la structure de la ville à cette époque et de mettre un visage sur les grands noms qui dominaient alors la scène canadienne.

Au-delà des témoignages physiques et architecturaux, les photographies de Notman évoquaient l'esprit de l'époque, le quotidien des années 1880 et 1890, avec sa technologie : lampes à gaz, tramways tirés par des chevaux, engins à vapeur, ses vêtements et ses coiffures. Autant d'indices qui levaient le voile sur les moeurs et les priorités économiques d'antan. C'est ce portrait de société, image inconsciemment figée par le photographe, qui présente au fil des années un intérêt et une valeur inestimables.

Cette recherche historique nous convainquit de l'importance de monter des archives photographiques qui illustreraient les villes canadiennes à la fin du XXe siècle. À l'époque de Notman, la photographie en était à ses balbutiements et, par conséquent, réservée au Canada à une poignée de photographes. C'est pourquoi ses photographies constituent à toute fin pratique les seuls documents visuels d'alors sur Montréal. Les appareils-photos étant de nos jours à la portée de presque tous, nous étions d'avis que les archives du XXe siècle devraient évoquer la vision personnelle de nombreux photographes. Privilégiant l'approche démocratique, les archives devaient refléter le point de vue des résidants mêmes de la ville, des quartiers. De nos jours, il n'est plus forcé, ni souhaité, que les archives présentent le point de vue d'un seul photographe.

Nous étions également intéressés à développer le concept d'animation urbaine, sortant la culture de ses tours d'ivoire et offrant à la population l'occasion de participer à la vie artistique et culturelle d'une ville. Mieux que toute autre forme d'art, la photographie favorisait cet objectif : accessible à la majorité, elle permet néanmoins d'exprimer des sentiments d'une intense complexité.

C'est ainsi que fut lancé notre premier projet, en 1982 : «Le Montréal des Montréalais», un concours photographique ouvert aux amateurs et aux professionnels, suivi d'une exposition de 400 photos agrandies et affichées dans les vitrines de la rue Sainte-Catherine, dans le centre-ville de Montréal. La rue, ainsi transformée en une vaste galerie en plein air, ouverte 24 heures sur 24, attira plus d'un million de personnes. Les archives photographiques créées à cette occasion furent offertes à la Ville de Montréal pour les générations à venir.

Depuis, les Projets photographiques urbains inc. ont organisé des événements semblables dans plusieurs autres villes :

Toronto en 1986, Montréal et San Diego en 1990, Vancouver et Ottawa en 1991.

Chacun de ces concours de photographies a donné lieu à une exposition publique en collaboration avec un lieu commercial central, ouvert et accessible gratuitement à la population. Ils ont également su intéresser un nombre croissant d'organismes culturels et d'entreprises privées, favorisant la rencontre fructueuse de nombreuses ressources de la ville. Enfin, chacun des projets a permis la création d'archives photographiques contemporaines comprenant épreuves et négatifs, qui ont été offertes à un service public ou à une société historique de la ville.

C'est de cette expérience qu'est née l'idée de «Visages du Canada». La photographie, selon nous, constituait un moyen parfait de célébrer le 125e anniversaire du Canada, sans risquer de tomber dans les problèmes constitutionnels, sociaux et autres qui secouent le pays à l'heure actuelle. Quelle meilleure façon de célébrer le Canada que de mettre en lumière ce qui rend ce pays si agréable à vivre : sa population ?

Le concours «Visages du Canada» a été lancé le 27 avril 1992, après plus d'un an de préparation. Ouvert à tous les Canadiens, photographes amateurs et professionnels, il ne comportait qu'une seule règle : montrer les Canadiens dans leur quotidien. À la clôture du concours, le 24 juillet 1992, 38 782 photographies nous étaient parvenues de tous les coins du pays.

De ce concours, trois produits verront le jour : ce livre, qui réunit 125 portraits; une exposition de 50 photographies,

qui fera le tour du pays d'octobre 1992 à décembre 1993; et des archives de 377 épreuves et négatifs, que Ford du Canada remettra au Musée canadien des civilisations.

Le but de «Visages du Canada» était de permettre à tous de participer à un événement culturel national, en hommage au 125e anniversaire du pays. L'avantage de la photographie est qu'elle ne comporte aucune barrière de langue, de culture, de classe, d'âge ni de genre, ce dont témoignent éloquemment les pièces soumises. Les Canadiens qui ne font pas de photographie pourront eux aussi participer à l'événement en venant découvrir l'exposition ou en se procurant ce livre.

Les portraits de ce livre ont été retenus en raison de leurs qualités et de leur représentativité de l'éventail de photos inscrites au concours. Ils n'ont pas été choisis selon la répartition géographique ou ethnique du pays, bien que vous y trouverez des visages de plusieurs régions et origines. Il a été clairement établi, dès le début, que le choix des photos ne devait pas servir à transmettre de message politique ni à énoncer quelque opinion que ce soit sur la situation actuelle. L'objectif était de créer une collection de portraits qui dépeindrait ce pays à la fin du XXe siècle. Les citations qui ponctuent le livre ont été choisies pour leur humour, afin de rappeler divers points de vue qui auront eu cours en cette période de notre histoire.

Nous espérons que vous aurez plaisir à découvrir ce collage de visages du Canada et que vous vous y reconnaîtrez.

ROBERT MARSHALL
DIRECTEUR ADJOINT

URBAN PHOTOGRAPHIC PROJECTS, INC.

Urban Photographic Projects, Inc. is a not-for-profit corporation formed by a small group of Canadians interested in creating photographic archives as a reference for future generations, and in the process, raise interest in photography as a popular art form.

This desire to create photographic archives grew out of an experience working on historical research in Montréal in the late 1970's. Individuals from the group made use of the McCord Museum's Notman Photographic Archives, a photographic record of Montréal taken by William Notman through the late 19th century. The Notman photographs were important to our work in piecing together the fabric of the city as it developed during the period as well as in giving a face to the individuals who played an important role in the development of Canadian society at the time.

Perhaps more important than the physical and architectural record provided by the Notman photographs is the sense of the era itself which was being recorded. The day to day reality of living in the 1880s and 1890s is captured in the photographs: we see the technology of the period – gas lamps, horse drawn street cars, steam engines – in daily use; the style of people's clothing and hair give intimate clues about social mores and economic priorities. It is this sense of captured time which is expressed through the photographic image, the unconscious aspects of the photograph, which take on an increasing value and interest over time.

As a result of this historic research project, a group of us were convinced of the importance of building photographic archives representing Canadian cities at the end of the 20th

century. When Notman was working in the 1880s and 1890s, photography was in its infancy and he was one of a small handful of photographers in Canada. For this reason, his photographs provide the only comprehensive visual record of Montréal in this period. Now, however, because most people have access to photographic equipment, we felt that 20th century archives should represent the individual views of many photographers. In a truly democratic sense, the archives should represent the photographer's view as a resident of the city and his own neighbourhood. It is no longer necessary or appropriate for archives of this kind to represent the point of view of a single photographer.

The group was also interested in the concept of urban animation – bringing culture out of the "palaces" and giving people an active role in the artistic and cultural life of their city. Photography is an ideal artistic form to achieve this objective because it is easily understood, accessible to everyone, yet is capable of great subtlety of expression and complexity of meaning.

The group's initial project was "Le Montréal des Montréalais" in 1982, a photographic competition open to both amateur and professional photographers. The competition resulted in an exhibition of 400 photographs, enlarged and exhibited in storefront windows along St. Catherine Street in downtown Montréal. The exhibition created a unique 24 hour open air gallery which drew well over a million people to the street for a popular cultural event. The photographic archives created by the project were donated to the City of Montréal Archives for the enjoyment and reference of future generations.

Since the Montréal project in 1982, Urban Photographic Projects, Inc. has been responsible for a number of similar competition, exhibition and archival projects in different cities including Toronto in 1986, Montréal and San Diego in 1990, Vancouver and Ottawa in 1991.

Each of the photographic competitions has involved a public exhibition in association with a downtown retail area, open and accessible at no charge to the general public. The events have also grown to involve a variety of cultural organizations and private businesses in their production, creating a context in which many city resources play together for mutual benefit. Each of the projects has also created a photographic archive of inter-negatives and prints which has been donated to an appropriate agency or historical society in the subject cities.

It was out of this experience that the concept for "Faces of Canada" was developed. We thought it would be appropriate to use photography as a means of celebrating the 125th Anniversary of Canada, avoiding the political and social morass of the constitutional debate and other issues currently affecting the country. What better way to celebrate Canada than to focus on its people – the individuals who make this country such a great place to live?

The "Faces of Canada" competition was launched on April 27, 1992, after more than a year of planning. The competition was open to all Canadians. The directive to both amateur and professional photographers was to enter photographic images of Canadians in the context of their everyday lives. By the time the competition closed on July 24, 1992, photographers had submitted 38,782 photographs from across the country.

Three products are being developed from the competition entries: this book, which contains 125 images; an exhibition of 50 photographs which will tour the country through 1993 and an archive of 377 inter-negatives and prints which

will be donated to the Canadian Museum of Civilization by the Ford Motor Company of Canada.

"Faces of Canada" was developed so that everyone could participate in a national cultural project celebrating the country's 125th Anniversary. Photographic competitions are interesting in that they allow everyone to participate regardless of language, cultural background, age or gender, and that range was reflected in the entries which were submitted for jurying. Even those Canadians who do not take photographs can participate in the event by attending the exhibition or enjoying this book.

The photographs in this book were selected because of their quality and because they are representative of the range and diversity of images received in the competition. Images were not selected on the basis of geographical distribution or ethnic representation, however, I am pleased to say that there are images from across the country with people of many different cultural backgrounds. The organizers clearly instructed the jury and the editors to avoid using the images to represent a particular political point of view or to make some kind of a statement on current issues. The objective has been to create a collection of images which give a combined sense of the character of the country at the end of the 20th century. The photos are full of humour, emotion and individual character. The quotations as well have been selected for their sense of humour, reflecting the diversity of opinion which colours this period in our nation's history.

We hope you will enjoy these varied faces of Canada and recognize something of yourself in this collage of individual images.

ROBERT MARSHALL
ASSOCIATE EDITOR

Producteur délégué :   J Marc Coté Pouliot

Directeur adjoint :   Robert Marshall

Collaborateur :   Christy McMillan

                            Peter Rudd

Recherchiste :   Heather Mullin

Comité de sélection :   Gary Beelik, Serge Clément,

                            J Marc Coté Pouliot, Robert Marshall,

                            Heather Mullin, Peter Rudd,

                            Karen Satok et Ingrid Saumart

Design graphique :   Spencer Francey Peters

Direction de la production : Clark Spencer

Direction artistique :   Paul Hodgson

Graphisme :   Karen Satok

Séparation de couleurs :   Linotext Digital Colour

Papier :   Phoenix Imperial blanc lustré 220m

                            Gracieuseté de Scheufelen N.A.

Distribution :   Papiers Inter-Cité

Reliure :   John Dyell Company

Typographie :   Perpetua

                            Lettrines françaises : Linoscript

                            Lettrines anglaises : Futura gras

Textes :   J Marc Coté Pouliot,

                            Robert Marshall, Krista Foss,

                            Peter Rudd et Heather Mullin

Textes français :   Monique Joly, L'écrit

Imprimé au Canada

La publication de Visages du Canada : collection de photographies Ford du Canada a été rendue possible grâce à la générosité de Ford du Canada, la Corporation Canada 125, Dylex limitée, Air Canada, Multiculturalisme et Citoyenneté Canada et Papiers Inter-Cité, et avec la collaboration de John Deyell Company, IPI Graphics et Linotext Digital Colour.

Pour leur appui et leurs conseils à la réalisation de ce livre, nous aimerions remercier tout spécialement Gregor Bingham, Rick Retter, Mark Gaudette, Reg Hunt et plus particulièrement Clark Spencer.

Executive Producer: J Marc Coté Pouliot

Associate Editor: Robert Marshall

Assistant to the Editor: Christy McMillan

Peter Rudd

Research Assistant: Heather Mullin

Editorial Committee: Gary Beelik, Serge Clément,

J Marc Coté Pouliot, Robert Marshall,

Heather Mullin, Peter Rudd,

Karen Satok and Ingrid Saumart

Graphic Design: Spencer Francey Peters

Production Management: Clark Spencer

Art Direction: Paul Hodgson

Design: Karen Satok

Colour Separations: Linotext Digital Colour

Paper: Phoenix Imperial Gloss White 220m

Compliments of Scheufelen N.A.

Canadian Distributor: Inter City Papers Group

Binding: John Deyell Company

Typeface: Perpetua

French drop cap: Linoscript

English drop cap: Futura Bold

Text: J Marc Coté Pouliot,

Robert Marshall, Krista Foss,

Peter Rudd and Heather Mullin

French Texts: Monique Joly, L'écrit

Printed in Canada

The publication of Faces of Canada: A Ford of Canada Photographic Collection was made possible through the generous assistance of the Ford Motor Company of Canada, the Canada 125 Corporation, the Dylex Corporation, Air Canada, Multiculturalism and Citizenship Canada, Inter City Papers and with the collaboration of the John Deyell Company, IPI Graphics and Linotext Digital Colour.

For their support and advice throughout the publishing process, we particularly want to thank Gregor Bingham, Rick Retter, Mark Gaudette, Reg Hunt and particularly Clark Spencer.

La seule culture digne d'être
conservée, c'est la
culture bactérienne. La vraie
culture, c'est une chose qu'on
s'efforce d'atteindre, pas quelque
chose qu'on met dans un pot
de marinades.

LOUIS DUDEK,
POETE ET PROFESSEUR DE
LITTÉRATURE ANGLAISE

The only culture you want
to preserve is bacterial.
Real culture is something you
strive to attain, not something
you keep in a pickle jar.

LOUIS DUDEK,
POET AND PROFESSOR OF
ENGLISH LITERATURE